CALYX
BOOKS

For Dianne —
warmly
Chitra B Dwakann

For Rianne –

warmly

Julia B. Gordon

Black Candle

The publication of this book was supported with grants from the National Endowment for the Arts and the Oregon Arts Commission.

Cover art by Louise LaFond
Cover design by Carolyn Sawtelle
Book design by Cheryl McLean

CALYX Books are distributed to the trade through major library distributors, jobbers, and most small press distributors, including: Airlift, Bookpeople, Bookslinger, The Distributors, Inland Book Co., Pacific Pipeline, and Small Press Distribution. For personal orders or other information, write: CALYX Books, PO Box B, Corvallis, OR 97339; (503) 753-9384.

The paper in this book meets the guidelines for permanence and durability of the Committee on Production Guidelines for Book Longevity of the Council on Library Resources and the minimum requirements of the American National Standard for the Permanence of Paper for Printed Library Materials Z38.48-1984.

Library of Congress Cataloging-in-Publication Data

Divakaruni, Chitra Banerjee, 1956-
    Black Candle : poems about women from India, Pakistan, and Bangladesh / Chitra Banerjee Divakaruni
      p. cm.
    ISBN 0-934971-24-2 (alk. paper): $16.95. —
    ISBN 0-934971-23-4 (pbk.): $8.95
    1. Women—India—Poetry. 2. Women—Pakistan—Poetry. 3. Women—Bangladesh—Poetry. I. Title.
    PS3554.I86B53   1991
    811'.54—dc20   91-29444
                                   CIP

Printed in the U.S.A.

Black Candle

Poems about Women from India,
Pakistan, and Bangladesh

Chitra Banerjee Divakaruni

CALYX Books
Corvallis, Oregon

Acknowledgements

The author gratefully acknowledges the Barbara Deming Memorial Award, which enabled her to complete this book manuscript. She also acknowledges the following publications in which these poems were previously published: "Bengal Night" in *Amelia* (forthcoming, 1991); "The Gift" in *Beloit Poetry Journal*, Vol. 40, No. 3, Spring 1990; "Bengal Night" and "The Robbers' Cave" in *Beloit Poetry Journal*, Vol. 38, No. 4, Summer 1988; "Journey" in *The California Quarterly* (forthcoming, 1991); "Mother and Child" and "The Rat Trap" in *CALYX, A Journal of Art and Literature by Women*, Vol. 12, No. 3, Summer 1990; "The Quilt" in *CALYX, A Journal of Art and Literature by Women*, Vol. 13, No. 2, Summer 1991; "Nargis' Toilette" and "Family Photo in Black and White" in *The Cape Rock*, Vol. 25, No. 1, Spring 1990; "Villagers Visiting Jodhpur Enjoy Iced Sweets" in *Chelsea*, Vol. 50, 1991; "In the Hinglaj Desert" in *The Colorado Review*, Vol. 15, No. 2, New Series, Winter 1988; "The Sati Temple," "Two Women Outside a Circus," and "The Arranged Marriage" in *Cream City Review*, Vol. 15, No. 1, Spring 1991; "Gouri Mashima" in *Embers*, Vol. 15, No. 2, Fall 1990; "Boychild" in *Folio*, Spring 1989; "Song of the Fisher Wife" in *Folio*, Fall 1991; "At Muktinath" in *The Forbidden Stitch, An Asian American Women's Anthology* (CALYX Books, 1989); "The Garba," "I, Manju," and "The Brides Come to Yuba City" in *India Currents*, Vol. 4, No. 3, June 1990; "Living Underground" and "My Mother Combs My Hair" in *International Poetry Review*, Vol. 16, No. 2, Fall 1990; "Sondra" and "Yuba City School" in *Looking for Home: Women Writing about Exile* (Milkweed Editions, 1990); "Burning Bride" and "My Mother at Maui" in *Primavera*, Vol. 11-12, 1988; "Making Samosas" in *Primavera*, Vol. 13, 1989; "The Room" and "Traitor Body" in *Santa Clara Review*, Vol. 77, No. 3, Spring 1990; "The Rainflies" in *The Threepenny Review*, Vol. 43, Spring 1990; "The Durga Batik" in *Woman of Power*, Winter 1990; "Visit" and "Sudha's Story" in *Woman of Power*, Fall 1990.

for
my mother

and
for
my sisters
of the
South Asian diaspora

TABLE OF CONTENTS

The Room

I have walked this corridor so many times
I no longer notice
the gouged floorboards, the brown light
washing the peeling walls, the stale
childhood smell of curried cabbage.

I am looking for the door,
the one whose striated knob
matches perfectly the lines of my palm,
which opens without sound
into a room with milk-blue walls.

On the sill, a brass bowl
of gardenias in water. Peacocks
spread silk feathers against cushions.
The white cockatoo on its stand
knows my name. Sun filters
through the *sari* of a woman
who rises toward me. I am caught
by the lines of her bones, the fine
lighted hairs on her held-out arm,
your eyes, mother, in her mouthless face.

Nargis' Toilette

*The uncovered face of a woman
is as a firebrand, inflaming men's
desires and reducing to ashes
the honor of her family.*
Muslim saying

Powder to whiten skin
unsnagged as a just-ripe peach.
Kohl to underline the eye's mute deeps.
Attar of rose touched to the dip
behind the earlobe,
the shadow between the breasts,
the silk creases
of the crimson *kameez*.

In the women's courtyard
it is always quiet,
the carved iron gates locked.
The palm shivers by the marble fountain.
The *bulbul* sings to its crimson double
in the mirrored cage.

Satin *dupattas* rustle.
The women put henna
on Nargis' hands. They braid,
down her back,
the forest's long shadows,
their laughter like the silver anklets
they are tying to her feet.

Today the women will take Nargis
to visit the women of the Amin family.
They will drink chilled pomegranate juice,
nibble pistachio *barfis* green as ice.
The grandmothers will chew
betel leaves and discuss the heat.
Nargis will sit, eyes down,
tracing the peacock pattern
on the mosaic floor.
If Allah wills, a marriage
will be arranged
with the Amins' second son
whose face Nargis will see
for the first time
in the square wedding mirror
placed in the bride's lap.

It is time to go.
They bring her *burkha*,
slip it over her head.
Someone adjusts the lace slits to her eyes.
The *burkha* spills silk-black to her feet
and spreads, spreads,
over the land, dark wave
breaking over the women, quenching
their light.

Now all is ready.
Like a black candle
Nargis walks to the gate.

Bengal Night

When foxes sing out behind
the bamboo grove and cranes' wings
whip the black air white,
the child stops her games
and fills a bucket at the pump
and washes. Water flows through
her hot fingers like moonlight,
leaching away the salt.
She plunges her face into it,
opening her mouth
to its cool, rusty taste.
On the verandah the aunt
cleans the lanterns, polishing
narrow chimney-glasses with a blue rag.
The child waits, breathing in
the kerosene smell. The aunt lights
the first lantern. The child sets out
to bring the grandfather home.

One lighted lantern into the night
swings great curved shadows on a path
red as the massy hibiscus on every side
where the child dreams green whiplash snakes
hanging like tendrils, their jewel eyes.
The claws of night lizards
skitter over rocks. Vapors rise
from the pocked phosphorus skin
of the mosquito swamp. Water insects
cry into the hearts of elephant-ears.

The child sets down the lantern,
its oval shell of light,
throws out her arms and whirls
around and around in the blue
breathless air. Her skirt
flares hibiscus-red to touch
the world. In the wheeling
sky, star-studded bats hang
motionless on great leather wings.

The Robbers' Cave

My favorite game was the one
where the robbers
slip into the palace at dead of night
and kidnap the princess of the snowy mountains
to become a prisoner in their cave
until the prince rescues her.
How I wanted to be princess.
But being seven, was always
the youngest robber,
the one who carries the rope
and, once the princess is tied up,
has nothing left to do.

The princess was a girl
whose black hair, at eleven,
already reached her swinging hips.
Her breasts pushed curiously
against the tight red *kameez*
her mother made her. My mother
was always pregnant, too tired
to make me anything.
Her hands blue-veined.
Her bone-bleached, bloodless face.
Father was a sour breath
exploding in sudden shouts,
punches to send us flying.
Nights I cried soundlessly
for my true father, lost at birth,
king of the snowy mountains.

The boy who was prince
had a silver sword his father
bought him at the fair. His eyes
were black lights. When he passed me
my heart leaped like a red fish
in my throat. We never spoke.

Not even on the day
the regular princess was sick
and I begged and begged until
they let me be princess
just once. I lay on the cool
cement floor of the cave,
not minding the rope
that numbed my wrists.
Breathed in the silent dark,
the odor of pickled mangoes
in large earth jars, waited
for the prince to roll away
the rock that stopped the cave-mouth.

He never came.
The pantry door was flung open
by Reba our maid
calling me to come home quick,
mother was dying.

The bed was full of blood. So much blood.
Ninth-month blood
and the baby, too, dying inside her,
trapped like a blind fish
in that black tidal cave.
Blood from her fractured skull
where he had flung her
against the stair wall.
The crack of bone, the heavy thud
of falling flesh
end over end into spiralled dark.
They tell me no one heard her scream.

In my dream I hear her. Again, again.
The scream ricochets off
the moist heaving walls
of the robbers' cave
where with tied wrists I swim
feebly against the pull
of the black tide,
insidious current sucking me under
like the metallic smell of her blood,
the burning breath
of father on me.

The prince never comes.

Gouri Mashima

From water country you came to a dry land,
a bride of fifteen. The walls of Calcutta
pressed black against your breathing.
Outside your window, in the wavering
heat, a dying tamarind tree. Pitch pavements
buckling like dry snakeskin. Inside,
seven in-laws to share the one bath.
Last in line, you never had enough,
scooped tepid handfuls from the cistern bottom.

In Rajhat, all day you used to swim with your
boy cousins. Diving, you wrapped yourself
in the river's brown skin. In underwater light,
water weeds fine as hair framed your face.
When you turned woman, morning and evening
with sisters and aunts you went
to the enclosed *ghats*. The women washed
each other's hair, picked red water-spinach
to carry home. Even that last day
you searched the river bottom for lotus roots.

Eight years of marriage. Your husband's
brothers' wives all bore children. Not you.
Bad luck to see your face, they said.
All day you worked in the kitchen, dim
with eye-burning smoke. Palms
cracked and yellow from grinding spices,
you leaned against the grimy wall,
listening to the years. In the rainless noon,
only the caged parrot called your name.

And the children. While our mothers slept,
we stole to you. You fed us forbidden
pickles, wiped tamarind stains
with callused fingers from our mouths.
Told us tales of rivers underground,
in whose waters lost princesses sleep.
One by one we left. Dry-eyed, you watched.

This summer, twenty years late, I
visit you. Calcutta is parched
with drought. Turned on, all day
the taps hiss, empty. Mornings,
half an hour, the water comes. We fill
every pot in the house, store water
in every room. Afternoons, windows
barred against the Baisakh blaze,
we lie on the floor. All around,
in earth jars, water trembles
in the humid breeze
from the tired ceiling fan.
I ask if you are happy.

You tell me of the river, the great
hay boats that floated slow by your house
each morning to Raniganj. How, at seven,
you hooked your arm into the looped
anchor-rope of a boat and let it take you.
By evening the land turned strange
and yellow. The trees had no names.
You swam ashore. The farmhand who found you

took you to his hut. His wife fed you
rice with green chilies. You lay
by her on the cool earth floor. Outside,
in dark, jackals called. The wings
of night birds rustled. You felt on your hair
her sleeping breath, like the river.

Next morning they sent you back
in a bullock cart. She tied
around your head a wet blue *sari*
to shield you from the sun. Gave you
chapatis wrapped in banana leaves,
buttermilk in an earth jar. Stood
at her door as long as you could see.
The bullocks ambled through mustard fields,
eye-watering bright. The driver dozed.
The jar was grainy-cool
against your mouth. You sipped
the sweet buttermilk all the way home.

The Rat Trap

after Adoor Gopalakrishnan's film Elippathayam

At night we sleep with the windows bolted
in spite of the sweat,
in the women's quarter,
elder sister and I.
The old house settles on my chest
like the grinding stone she uses each day
to make chili paste. My pale hands
burn my body.
Outside I can hear the *Kaju* trees
growing, green poison, toward the house.
Today, again, brother
refused an offer for elder sister's marriage:
Not good enough
for our family name.
Now from the main room, he frog-snores,
while night leaches the black from her hair,
cracks open the edges of her eyes.

I wait for the rat. In the passage
the coconut sliver I hooked into the trap
is a thin white smile, moon
to my dark nights. Soon,
the clatter of the wooden slat falling,
the shrill squeaks, the frantic
skittering claws. Then silence.

In the morning, the huge eyes, glint-black,
will watch me as I carry the cage
through palms whose jagged leaves
splinter the sky.
Monsoon mud sucks at my feet. The pink,
hairless tail twitches. The green pond
closes over my wrist.
The cage convulses, quiets.
A few bubbles, stillness.
I know how it is.
I open the trapdoor. The limp brown body
thuds onto the ash heap
next to the others. The red ants swarm.
I watch and watch, then run
all the way home.

After bath, in front of the great gilt mirror,
grandmother's wedding dowry,
elder sister combs the wet dark
down my back. I press on my forehead,
for luck, vermillion paste
like a coin of blood,
check my white teeth.
They look smaller, sharper, rodent-honed.
Our eyes meet, glint-black, in the smoky mirror.
Red ants swarm up my spine.

The Arranged Marriage

The night is airless-still, as
before a storm. Behind the wedding drums,
cries of jackals from the burning grounds.
The canopy gleams, color
of long life, many children.
Color of bride-blood. At the entrance
the women have painted the sign
of Laxmi, goddess of wealth, have put up
a blackened pot to ward off
the witch who lives beyond
the *Sheora* forest and eats
young flesh.
             Guests from three villages
jostle, make marriage jokes. A long
conch blast for the groom's party,
men in *dhotis* white as ice. Someone runs to them
with water of rose, silvered betel leaves,
piled garlands from which rise
the acrid smell of marigolds.
The priests confer, arrange wood and incense
for the wedding fire. The chants begin.
Through smoke, the stars
are red pinpricks, the women's voices
almost a wailing. Uncles and brothers
carry in the bride, her face hidden
under an edge of scarlet silk, her trembling
under the wedding jewels.

        The groom's father
produces his scales and in clenched silence
the dowry gold is weighed. But he smiles
and all is well again. Now it is *godhuli*,
the time of the auspicious seeing.
Time for you, bride of sixteen,
mother, to raise the tear-stained face
that I will learn so well,
to look for the first time into
your husband's opaque eyes.

The Living Goddess Speaks

Kathmandu, Nepal

He had been there always, the old man
hovering at the edges of my childhood.
His shaven head, his white priest's robe.
Between games of tag and doll weddings
he darted, dry, lizard-leathery.
Following my sister home from the bazaar
I would feel his eyes on me.
His soundless lips moving.

My fifth birthday, he came into the house, spoke
to grandfather. I was brought in, examined:
forehead, palms, the soles of my feet.
Yes, I had the thirty-two auspicious signs. I must
be taken to the temple, must become
Kumari, the new Living Goddess. A great honor.
I clung to mother. They pried my fingers loose.
Gently. The Living Goddess must not be harmed.

Like mist they haze past,
the nights alone in the ivory bed,
the noises. The days on the temple throne,
the high chill silver seat, the gold-worked silks.

The jewels pulling at my throat.
Garlands, incense, nightmare toll
of bells. Dying babies thrust at my feet.
The lame, the blind, the mad.
I saw, touched all. Knew names
of all diseases, though often not
the meaning. Early I learned
the Living Goddess does not ask, or weep.

One day they brought my sister. In her stiff
bride-silks she touched her forehead
to my feet for blessing.
A burning shuddered through me. I could
say nothing. The Living Goddess does not speak.

Seven years. Any day now my blood's dark flow
will bring release. They do not tell me, but
I know, already they have found my successor.
What life for me beyond these walls,
these iron doors? Even my attendant women,
bringing bath water or evening lamps,
shrink from my gaze. The final clang
of the gates behind me, who will I find
to part the lips that have learned not to speak?

Who can kiss shut the eyes that cannot weep?
Or lower his weight between the open legs
of a once Living Goddess?

Evenings at my window, up on tiptoe,
pressed against the bars, I hear bazaar women
selling candy, shiny red and green,
jewel bright. Below, the brown canal
where temple offerings are thrown.
Dying jasmines from my coronet, crushed
hibiscus from my throat, my feet.
They swirl by slow, then fast, faster,
into the vortex of a river
dark, rushing, somewhere beyond my sight.

Note: The worship of the Living Goddess continues even today in
Kathmandu, Nepal. The "goddesses" are discarded at puberty.
Feared and avoided, they live out their lives as outcasts.

Mother and Child

At last the wrench,
    the tearing loose in the belly
after the dragged day
    long with heat and flies
and her eyes from the floor
trying to hold the midwife's sweaty face,
discolored teeth chewing *paan*.

The knife grinds in the loins.
In the banyan
the crowsounds die
and the failing sun
is blood in her eyes.

In the corner around the oil lamp
the women, led by the grandmother,
are praying for a safe birth, a boy,
as at her last labor, now a thin bile-taste
in her mouth.
Their voices shatter against her,
insistent, like the thought
    of the dead one.

They would not let her
see the body
but in her dreams
she follows it, bloated,
down the dark river
where it was cast.

Her lungs jerk out a scream.
She tries to suck in air.
Inside, sudden emptiness,
the blood warm on thighs,
familiar as tears. She strains
for the life-sound, cry of her flesh,
but the coconut trees rustle so loudly
she cannot hear.

Above her, distended faces
swinging like pendulums,
women-wails rising
dark like the river.

She tries to rise on her elbow.
The lamp's hard yellow eye,
hot kerosene smell, nausea,
thoughts of empty days, pointed fingers
there goes the childless one
endless blind nights under his sweaty body.

Easier to let the breath go now,
slip into the shadow
beyond the burning light,
the voices,
to travel the river
with her faceless child.

Song of the Fisher Wife

He pushes out the boat, black skeleton
against the pale east. His veins
are blue cords. Sun scours the ocean
with its red nails. I hand him
curds and rice wrapped in leaves. Sand
wells over my feet, rotting smell
of seaweed. I sing with the wives.

> *O husbands, muzzle the great wave,*
> *leap the dark. Bring back boats*
> *filled with fish like silver smiles,*
> *silver bracelets for our arms.*

All day I dry the fish, the upturned eyes,
the dead, grinning jaws. How stiff
flesh feels, the flaking layers
under my hand. Salt has cracked
my palms open. The odor crusts me.
My eyes are flecked with sand
and waiting. How well I learn
by the dryness in my mouth
to tell the coming storm.

> *O husbands, no fear*
> *though the sky's breath is black.*
> *We line the calling shore, faithful.*
> *Lip and eye and loin, we keep you*
> *from the jagged wind.*

They say all heard the crack and yell,
the boat exploding into splintered air.
Searched for hours. They strip
my widowed arms, shave off my hair.
Thrust me beyond the village walls.
Nights of no-moon they will come to me,
grunting, heaving, grinding
the damp sand into my naked back,
men with cloths over their faces.

> *O husband, sent by my evil luck*
> *into the great wave's jaw,*
> *do you ride the ocean's boiling back,*
> *eyes phosphorus, sea-lichen hair, gleam*
> *of shell-studded skin, to see*
> *my forehead branded whore?*

Note: In many coastal villages in India, it is believed that the wife's
virtue keeps her husband safe at sea. Widows are often outcast and
forced into becoming prostitutes in order to survive.

My Mother Tells Me a Story

First you were
big as a mustard seed,
sputtering light,
then a starapple, tart-shining,
a persimmon
with the blood's own glow,
a pomelo, green and growing
as breath.

Then large as the muskmelons
behind eldest cousin's house,
you pushed against my heartbeat,
girlchild,
the invisible frostmark of your sex
already on you.

It was *Diwali* night in my father's house,
everywhere firecrackers,
lamps and demons.
I felt the water explode
in me like a fear.
I screamed for your grandmother,
all the lights went blue.
The *ayah* was waiting with the knife.
The women chanted loud
to keep the demons away.

The hours flowed out of me,
they were bright and sharp as glass.
They drained out of me,
pale and flickering.
When they were all gone,
someone put you on my breast.
They covered us with a yellow quilt
for luck,
they called the men.

My father came to see,
my three brothers came,
they tucked coins into your fists,
they said you had my eyes.

No one could find your father.

For days afterward the house
would smell of blood
like the birthrags burning.

Two Women Outside a Circus, Pushkar

after a photograph by Raghubir Singh

Faces pressed to the green stakes
of the circus fence, two village women,
red-veiled, with babies,
crouch low in the cloudy evening
breathing in the odors of the strange beasts
painted on the canvas above:
great black snakes with ruby eyes,
tigers with stars sewn onto their skins.
Beyond, a tent translucent with sudden light,
bits of exotic sound: gunshots, a growl,
a woman's raucous laugh.

The Nepal Circus demands
five rupees for entry to its neon world
of bears that dance, and porcupines
with arm-long poison quills. But five rupees
is a sack of *bajra* from Ramdin's store,
a week's dinner for the family. So the women
look and look
at the lighted sign of the lady acrobat.

In a short pink sequined skirt
she walks a tightrope
over gaping crocodile-jaws, twirling
her pink umbrella. Inside the tent,
the crowd shrieks as Master Pinto the Boy Wonder
is hurled from a flaming cannon. The women
clutch each other and search the sky

for the thunder-sound. Ecstatic applause.
The band plays a hit from *Mera Naam Joker*
and the crowd sings along.

The women gather their babies
and head home to the canvas of their lives:
endless coarse *rotis*
rolled in smoky kitchens, slaps or caresses
from husbands with palm-wine breaths, whining,
clutching children and more in the belly, perhaps
a new green skirt at harvest time.

But each woman
tending through burning noon the blinkered bull
that circles, all day, the *bajra*-crushing stones,
or wiping in dark the sweat
of unwanted sex from her body, remembers
in sparkling tights the woman acrobat
riding a one-wheeled cycle so immense
her head touches the stars. Remembers
the animal trainer in her leopard skins,
holding a blazing hoop through which leap
endless smiling lions.

Note: *Mera Naam Joker:* a popular movie featuring circus
performers

The Quilt

The parrot flies to the custard-apple tree.
The bees are among the pomegranates.
I call and call you, little bride.
Why do you not speak?
Bengali Folk Song

Blue and sudden as beginning,
a quilt at the bottom
of the small mahogany chest
which holds her things.

She died in childbirth,
this grandmother whose name
no one can tell me.

He married again,
a strong woman this time,
straight backed, wide-hipped
for boy-children.
In the portrait downstairs
she wears the family diamonds
and holds her fourth son.

There are no pictures
of the wife who failed.

Her quilt leaves on my fingers
satin dust
as from a butterfly wing.

I spread it against
the floor's darkness, see her fingers
working it into the world-design,
the *gul-mohur* tree
bright yellow against the blue,
the river winding through rice fields
into a horizon where men with swords
march to a war
or a wedding.

As the baby grew she stitched in
a drifting afternoon boat
with a peacock sail.
In the foreground, young grass.
A woman with a deer.
She is left unfinished,
no eyes, no mouth,
her face a smooth blankness
tilted up at birds
that fall like flames from the sky.

At the Sati Temple, Bikaner

after a photograph by Raghubir Singh

The sun is not yet up. In early light
the twenty-six handprints on the wall
glisten, pink as beginning. The priest
has sprinkled them with holy water, pressed
kumkum into the hollow of each cool palm,
the red of married bliss. The handprints
are in many sizes, large for grown women,
small for childbrides, all *satis*
who burned with their husbands' bodies.
They have no names, no stories
except what the priest tells each day
to women who have traveled the burning desert
on bare, parched feet.

> *...they threw themselves on the blazing pyres*
> *tearing free of restraining hands,*
> *flowers fell from heaven,*
> *sacred conch sounds drowned the weeping,*
> *the flames flew up into the sky,*
> *the handprints appeared on the temple wall...*

The women jostle each other, lift
dusty green veils for a closer look. Untie
coins from a knotted *dupatta* so the priest
will pray for them to the *satis*.
The young girls want happy marriages, men
who will not beat them. The older ones
ask cures for female diseases, for
a husband's roving eye. The priest

29

hands them vermillion paste in a *shal* leaf,
the *satis'* blessing. The women
kneel, foreheads to flagstones,
begin the long way home.

Sand wells up hot and yellow
around their ankles. Sun sears
their shoulders. No one speaks.
Each woman carries, tucked in her *choli*,
the blessing which she will put, for luck,
under her wedding mattress. Carries
on the heart's dark screen
images that pulse like lightning.

> *...girlbodies dragged to flames, held down*
> *with poles, flared eyes, mouths*
> *that will not stop, thrash, hiss*
> *of hair, skin bubbling away*
> *from pale pink underflesh...*

Behind, the *Lu* wind starts. Dust
stings through thin veils. The temple wavers,
pink in the gritty air. In this place
of no words, the women walk and walk.
Somewhere in the blind sand,
a peacock's cry, harsh, cut-off,
for its mate or for rain.

Note: Although the practice of *sati*, the burning of widows on their husbands' funeral pyres, was outlawed in India in the nineteenth century, isolated incidents of *sati* still occur and *Sati* temples extolling the virtue of the burned wives continue to flourish.

The Brides Come to Yuba City

The sky is hot and yellow, filled
with blue screaming birds. The train
heaved us from its belly
and vanished in shrill smoke.
Now only the tracks
gleam dull in the heavy air,
a ladder to eternity, each receding rung
cleaved from our husbands' ribs.
Mica-flecked, the platform
dazzles, burns up through thin
chappal soles, lurches
like the ship's dark hold,
blurred month of nights, smell of vomit,
a porthole like the bleached iris
of a giant unseeing eye.

Red-veiled, we lean into each other,
press damp palms, try
broken smiles. The man
who met us at the ship whistles
a restless *Angrezi* tune
and scans the fields. Behind us,
the black wedding trunks, sharp-edged,
shiny, stenciled with strange men-names
our bodies do not fit into:
Mrs. Baldev Johl, Mrs. Kanwal Bains.
Inside, folded like wings,
bright *salwar kameezes* scented
with sandalwood. For the men,
kurtas and thin white gauze
to wrap their uncut hair.

Laddus from Jullundhar, sugar-crusted,
six kinds of lentils, a small bag
of *bajra* flour. Labeled in our mothers'
hesitant hands, pickled mango and lime,
packets of seeds —*methi, karela, saag*—
to burst from this new soil
like green stars.

He gives a shout, waves
at the men, their slow
uneven approach. We crease our eyes
through the veils' red film,
cannot breathe. Thirty years
since we saw them. Or never,
like Harvinder, married last year
at Hoshiarpur to her husband's photo,
which she clutches tight to her
to stop the shaking. He is fifty-two,
she sixteen. Tonight —like us all—
she will open her legs to him.

The platform is endless-wide.
The men walk and walk
without advancing. Their lined,
wavering mouths, their
eyes like drowning lights.
We cannot recognize a single face.

Note: Yuba City in northern California was settled largely by Indian railroad workers around the 1900s. Due to immigration restrictions, many of them were unable to bring their families over — or, in the case of single men, go back to get married — until the 1940s.

Yuba City School

From the black trunk I shake out
my one American skirt, blue serge
that smells of mothballs. Again today
Neeraj came crying from school. All week
the teacher has made him sit
in the last row, next to the fat boy
who drools and mumbles,
picks at the spotted milk-blue
skin of his face, but knows
to pinch, sudden-sharp,
when she is not looking.

The books are full of black curves,
dots like the eggs the boll-weevil lays
each monsoon in furniture-cracks
in Ludhiana. Far up in front
the teacher makes word-sounds
Neeraj does not know. They float
from her mouth-cave, he says,
in discs, each a different color.

Candy-pink for the girls
in their lace dresses, matching
shiny shoes. Silk-yellow
for the boys beside them,
crisp blond hair, hands raised
in all the right answers. Behind them
the Mexicans, whose older brothers,
he tells me, carry knives,
whose catcalls and whizzing rubber bands

clash, mid-air, with the teacher's
voice, its sharp purple edge.
For him, the words are
a muddy red, flying low and heavy,
and always the one he has learned to understand:
idiot, idiot, idiot.

I heat the iron over the stove. Outside
evening blurs the shivering
in the eucalyptus. Neeraj's shadow
disappears into the hole
he is hollowing all afternoon.
The earth, he knows, is round, and if
one can tunnel all the way through,
he will end up in Punjab,
in his grandfather's mango orchard,
his grandmother's songs lighting
on his head, the old words
glowing like summer fireflies.

In the playground, Neeraj says,
invisible hands snatch at his uncut hair,
unseen feet trip him from behind,
and when he turns, ghost laughter
all around his bleeding knees.
He bites down on his lip
to keep in the crying. They are
waiting for him to open his mouth,
so they can steal his voice.

I test the iron with little drops of water
that sizzle and die. Press down
on the wrinkled cloth. The room fills
with a smell like singed flesh.
Tomorrow in my blue skirt I will go
to see the teacher, my tongue
stiff and swollen
in my unwilling mouth, my few
English phrases. She will pluck them
from me, nail shut my lips. My son
will keep sitting in the last row
among the red words that drink his voice.

Note: The boy in the poem is a Sikh immigrant, whose religion
forbids the cutting of his hair.

Mother cried a lot, nights. I would wake and her muted sobs would hit me, wave after wave, till I could no longer tell where the sounds were coming from and felt like I was drowning in the narrow boatlike bed we shared. At first I would sit up and ask, what is it, *Amma*, where does it hurt? Very softly, of course. We both knew what would happen if we woke father who slept in the next room. But my question only made her lunge for me and crush my face to her breasts and cry even more, her entire body shuddering with the force of it. The damp smell of talcum powder and *sari* starch would fill the hollows of my body—stomach and chest and skull—till I couldn't breathe and had to push her away, and that of course made things worse. So I learned to lie rigid and unmoving at the farthest edge of the bed, the air pressing down on my body like an iron sheet, my mouth flooding with the tartness that comes just before throwing up. I would clamp my teeth hard and dig my nails into my palms to keep it in, so that in the morning my jaw would hurt all the way to the back of my neck and there would be a line of red marks like new moons across my palms. When it got real bad I would hold my breath and squeeze my eyelids till little pinpricks of fire danced across them. If I held on long enough, the pinpricks turned into red and purple blotches, just like the pictures in my book about sea creatures, and I could pretend for a little while that I was in the ocean among the anemones.

We never spoke of it during the day. Mother was so efficient, so *mother* as she swept and washed and chopped and fixed meals and sent me off to school or to the park, I didn't know how. The one time I did ask, a day when she was in a good mood, letting me shell peas with her, she looked me straight in the eye and said she didn't know *what* I was talking about and sent me to bed without dinner because little girls mustn't let their imaginations run amuck. I went without protest although my stomach hurt with hunger and dinner that night was *matar-panir* curry, which I loved. In the bedroom I lay and looked at the pictures made by the cracks in the ceiling-plaster, quite happy, really, because now I knew that it must be all in my head, like the hairy ape-creature who sometimes waited in the shadowy hallway when I went to the bathroom, who would clamp his huge callused palm on my mouth, and pull me into the next room, groping, dribbling hot man-slobber all over my body. And that night, though she sobbed and sobbed till the whole bed shook, I didn't wake up at all.

I, Manju

after Mira Nair's film Salaam Bombay!

1.

The bed smells of crushed jasmine,
my mother's hair,
the bodies of strange men.
All day she lies
against the pillow's red velvet.
Smoke rings fly up, perfect ovals
from her shining mouth. Sometimes
she tells me shadow-stories,
butterfly fingers
held against the light.
On the panes, silver snakes
of rain. The curtains
flap their wild wet wings.
My friend the tea boy
brings us sweet steaming *chai*
from the shop below.
She lets me drink from her glass,
wipes the wet from his hair.
Turns up the radio. A song
spills into us.
She claps in time and laughs.
We dance and dance
around the bed
as though the rainbow music
will never end.

2.

From the balcony, my waiting
probes the swollen night.
Like light down a tunnel
she disappears into the room,
each time with a different
man. My fingers
squeeze the rails
till rust scars the palms.
The door shuts. The curtains
shiver with the silhouettes.
My nails are cat-claws
on the panes. Tinkle of glass,
a sharp curse, thick men-sounds
like falling.
After a long time
my feet find the way
to the street-children.
They let me lie with them
on newspaper beds,
do not ask. My face tight
against the tea boy's
cool brown spine. My arms.
I, Manju. All the dark
burns with the small animal sounds
from my mother's throat.

Traitor Body

I bend into dark furrowed soil,
press down seedlings, their pale, hairy roots.
Warm earth closes over my fingers
moist as a mouth, a womb. When I look up,
the horizon tilts and plunges, the sky
blinds me with its blazing. There is nothing
to hold onto.

       In the river the women
are bathing Nitin the blacksmith's wife
in celebration of her third month.
They have brought yellow chrysanthemums
and betel nuts, vermillion paste
(may she keep her husband happy),
turmeric (may it be a successful birth,
a boy).

       Red spinach lines the river
in clumps, blue water-hyacinths where
iridescent long-legs nest. He first
saw me bathing, filling
my brass pitcher, wringing out
my wet *sari*, the water skin-warm,
curling around the waist
like a lover's touch.

       When he spoke
I knew I should leave, but my body
opening under his eye like a lotus
would not listen. Nights my feet

betrayed me, stepping silent to him
past my sleeping mother. Moonlit,
the ricefields shone a silent warning
when he drew me down in shadow.
My disobedient lips parted under his.
Haystacks whispered in wind,
the night birds cried my fate. My eyes
were deaf to all except
his whirlwind breath.

     Now the women
sing the joy of mothers. Their conch-calls
shrill into me. I stand
ankle deep in mud in this unending field,
my girlhood shattered. My mouth
is bitter bile. Two months back
the blood stopped. There is no one
to tell this throbbing that I cannot check,
this silent, swollen growth.

     The women
are tying to her arm a brass amulet
on a black thread against the evil eye
(may she never bring shame on her house).
Soon they will pass this way, offering
sweet *laddus*. Out of this body's chasm
I will smile back, drag up
the words of luck, open my hands
for their gift.

                    Later
when the moon turns cold red
and jackals have stopped crying
under the banyan, I will go
to the river. It will not be too hard
to push away the hyacinths, to tie
the brass pitcher to my waist.
Wade in neck-deep and feel
the sudden lift of water, the limbs
weightless. My *sari* spreading about me,
a night-blooming magnolia. Kick out
till the current catches and pulls
like his hands. I will not think
of water burning lungs, thrash
of rebel arms and legs, the going under.
Only what is left: silent light,
smooth skin of river, this last winning
over the traitor body.

The Garba

The nine sacred nights of *Navaratri*
we dance the *Garba*. Light glances
off the smooth wood floor of the gym
festooned with mango leaves
flown in from Florida. The drummers
have begun, and the old women
singing of Krishna and the milkmaids.
Their high keening is an electric net
pulling us in, girls who have never seen

the old land. This October night
we have shed our jeans
for long red skirts, pulled back
permed hair in plaits, stripped off
nailpolish and mascara, and pressed
henna onto hands, kohl
under the eyes. Our hips
move like water to the drums.
Thin as hibiscus petals, our skirts
swirl up as we swing and turn.
We ignore the men,

creaseless in bone-white kurtas.
In the bleachers, they smile behind their hands.
Whisper. Our anklets shine
in the black light from their eyes.
Soon they will join us in the *Dandia* dance.
The curve and incline, the slow arc
of the painted sticks meeting red on black
above our upraised arms. But for now

the women dance alone,
a string of red anemones
flung forward and back
by an unseen tide. The old ones sing
of the ten-armed goddess.
The drums pound faster
in our belly. Our feet glide
on smooth wood, our arms
are darts of light. Hair, silver-braided,
lashes the air like lightning.
The whirling is a red wind
around our thighs. Dance-sweat
burns sweet on our lips.
We clap hot palms like thunder. And

the mango branches grow into trees.
Under our flashing feet,
the floor is packed black soil.
Damp faces gleam and flicker in torchlight.
The smell of harvest hay
is thick and narcotic
in our throat. We spin and spin
back to the villages of our mothers' mothers.
We leave behind

the men, a white blur,
like moonlight on empty *bajra* fields
seen from a speeding train.

Sudha's Story

*I lean into my knee and twine
my glowing fingers
in the* Alarippu.
*I lift my curved neck to the sky.
My body is a lotus. I dance open
in the rays from your eyes.*

1.

He saw her first at the Festival.
Flaming in scarlet silk
she danced the *Tillana*
unfaltering. The tabla played faster.
Her braid whipped the air,
black lightning, as she spun. Her feet
were a blur of light. The people
could not stop clapping.

He sent word through the matchmaker.
Her parents were delighted. An officer
at Delhi, and she a small-town girl,
not even out of college. They sold
the village home for a grand
wedding. All the relatives came.

In the bride-bedroom
he asked her to dance.
As she swayed, arms raised,
in the love dance of *Radha*,
he turned her to him, wound the braid

around her throat.
From now on, you dance
only for me.
His lips kissed shut
the surprise in her eyes.

2.

On honeymoon at the Taj Mahal,
he laughed at her delight
in the translucent tombs
and pulled her close. But at night
his fingers tightened on her naked shoulders.
I saw how you looked at the guide,
how you smiled.
Next day he took her home.

He told her to put away her textbooks.
He knew what went on in college.
All those young women
flirting with men.
Not my wife.

Each morning, leaving for work,
he locked her in. All day
she walked the large house, room
by room by room. Leaned her head
against the windowbars to cool the burn.
Evenings, he brought gifts —
a new *sari*, perfume —
made her wear them to bed.

Her parents' letters were full of praise.
A promotion already, such
a generous husband, all the relatives
are dying of envy. She crushed
them in her fists, did not reply.
Nights she dreamed escape, body
swinging limp-necked on a rope
from a huge hook in the ceiling.
When she woke, the ceiling
stretched above her, endless,
always empty.

3.

When he found her throwing up,
mornings, he laughed and crushed
her to his chest. *Now my mark's*
on you, in you, bearing my name.
He filled her nightstand with vitamins,
took her to the best doctors.
Let her sleep alone. Her belly
rounded, pulsed in a silver haze.
Days and nights spun away.

Until he flung the test results
on her face. *This isn't*
my child. No one in my family
fathered girl-children, ever. Tell me who
you slept with, who.
He left her on the floor.

The crack of the door-bolt
ricocheted a long time in her skull.

That night the tonic tasted strange.
She woke retching,
doubled with cramps. Pain
jabbed at her belly
like broken glass. Poison,
she thought, then felt the blood,
its thin sticky flow.
He watched from the door, eyes
like dead moons. Next day
he sent her parents
a regret telegram.

When his sleeping breath rasped
the dark, she stole to his bedroom door,
bolted it from outside. Poured
the cooking kerosene.
From her wedding-trunk, she shook out
her dance costume: gold anklets,
red silk. The flames took
the curtains and chairs,
moved their mouths along the carpet.
She began the *Nataraja*,
dance for the world's burning end.

My right foot balances
on a wheel of fire.
I swing the left across
the trembling air.
My palm holds up the sky,
which will fall
when I turn my wrist. The drums
die away. In the black quiet,
only the flames.
Blood streaked, they whisper to me
in my daughter's voice.

Note: The *Alarippu, Tillana,* and *Nataraja* are classical Indian dances.
The *Alarippu* usually occurs at the beginning of a performance, the
Nataraja at the end.

The Makers of Chili Paste

The old fort on the hill
is now a chili factory
and in it, we
the women,
saris tied over nose and mouth
to keep out the burning.

On the bare brown ground
the chilies are fierce hills
pushing into
the sky's blue. Their scarlet
sears our sleep.
We pound them into powder
red-acrid as the mark
on our foreheads.

All day the great wood pestles
rise and fall,
rise and fall,
our heartbeat. Red
spurts into air, flecks our arms
like grains of dry blood.
The color will never
leave our skins.

We are not like the others
in the village below,
glancing bright black
at men
when they go to the well for water.

Our red hands
burn like lanterns
through our solitary nights.
We will never
lie breathless
under the weight of thrusting men,
birth bloody children.

We are the makers of chili paste.
Through our fingers
the mustard oil seeps
a heavy, melted gold. In it
chili flecks swirl and drown.
We mix in secret spices,
magic herbs,
seal it in glowing jars
to send throughout the land.

All who taste our chilies
must dream of us,
women with eyes like rubies,
hair like meteor showers.
In their sleep forever
our breath will blaze
like hills of chilies
against a falling sun.

Sondra

You stock the shelves with quick-food—baked beans, canned peas, chips, mini-boxes of Kellogg's cornflakes imported for American tourists—standing on tiptoe to reach the top, pulling at the short red skirt which rides up your thigh. He bought it for you when he opened the store. Bring in more folks, he said.

Outside, bougainvillaeas explode magenta against a December sky thick with sea-smell and Christmas bells from St. James. All the other stores are closed today. More business for us, he said. You fluff out your frizzed hair and aim a smile at the small mirror on the wall by the cash register where Robbie and Nicky's photo is taped. You hope they're keeping out of trouble, out of their daddy's way, maybe mucking out the coops so you won't have to do it when you get home. You—he—owns a chicken farm, and the brown eggs which you fondle, warm on the counter, are from birds you have named. Mary, Linda, Suzie—and Gulabi, from a story your grandmother used to tell you. But you don't want to think about Gulabi because you fed her corn out of your palm, but then she stopped laying, and when you came home from the store he had already wrung her neck, and you had to pluck her and cook her although you threw up in the sink twice. Pound her, because the meat was tough, and cook her and make her into kabobs to sell the next day.

Once your name was Sundari, meaning beautiful, and your parents' love wound tight and dark around you like the roots of the giant banyan growing over your house in

Trinidad. But when they started writing home for bride-grooms, mailing your picture and horoscope and dowry agreements back to India, you had to go. With a coal-skinned, casteless man, a *chamar*, they called him. They performed a purification *puja* and never mentioned you again, never replied to your letters from Barbados. Not when the first child came with its black crinkly hair, not when he left you for the lead limbo dancer at the Apple Experience, and you sick and throwing up with the other one who luckily died. Not when you had to go work at the Roti Hut leaving Robbie with the landlady although you suspected she was giving him something in his sugarwater to keep him quiet, while the smell of curry took your clothes and hair, and your skin stank of it no matter how much you scrubbed.

And then the white man with the cracked-eggshell eyes every day at the Roti Hut, watching you silently. When you got off work his rickety Volkswagen was so much better than sway-standing on the bus trying to push away the sweaty bodies pressing into you. Then his unmade bed with the sheets smelling faintly of chicken feathers and the crickets crying in the walls, his weight thrusting down, tearing in, his big man-hands gripping you after so, so long. The morning sickness started and you moved in, which was a good thing for both of you, because you cleaned up the place and cooked and did his laundry and saved him money and kept him from the drink at least some of the time. And he gave you a safe place to stay, an almost-home, a body to hold onto through the quicksand nights.

He let the children call him daddy and was mostly kind and hardly ever took his belt to them as long as you all disappeared when his white friends came by.

And now, the store with its creamy-clean shelves gleaming with multicolored cans, the little glass-topped counter stocked with your own kabobs and *rotis*. The freezer hidden in the back with the illegal beer that the workmen so love, coming in from the blazing midday calling you pretty lady, brown sugar, darlin', stroking you in your short red skirt with their hot eyes and letting you keep the change if it isn't too much. And recently he's been saying if the business keeps up, in three, maybe two years, he'll take you and the kids to Florida, to Disney World. You know what's in Disney World. The woman who owns the laundry service down on Hastings Main Road went there last year. She's told you all about them — Mickey and Minnie, the Singing Bears, the boat ride through fire and water in the pirates' cave, the tallest, fastest rollercoaster in the world which pulls your screaming stomach up into your dry mouth, the room filled with snowflakes where you become tiny, tiny, tiny, until you disappear. You know them all, and you say them to yourself in that high singsong voice that is for Nicky's bedtime, as you caress the eggs, their frail brown skins, with a bougainvillaea finger, standing in the middle of the empty shop waiting for customers while darkness drops around you like a net.

Making Samosas

We sift salt into *chapati* flour, pour oil
and skin-warm water. *Punch it*
more, more, my mother says. *The trick*
is to get all the kinks out
before you start. The filling
is already cooling, spread on
the round tin tray on the counter
where this winter day the late sun
catches it briefly, the warm yellow
potatoes, the green glint of peas. She
rolls out the dough that I have made
into little balls, her circles perfect

as in my childhood. *The doctor said*
he wasn't to have any, she says.
But what rages he would fly into
if we tried to stop him. Remember
that time on your birthday
when he threw the chutney bowl
clear across the room?
My father, whom we have not seen
these seven years
who hung up each time we called

even after his stroke. I stir
tamarind into the chutney and see him
as she does,
in his kitchen 1500 miles away,
his left leg dragging a little.
He peers into the leached white light

of a refrigerator, reaches for
a carton, a bottle. Around him
a city of silent, falling snow.
Stuff carefully, she says, *press too hard
and they'll fall apart.* The oil ready,

she slides the samosas in, one by one.
They puff up crisp and golden,
hissing. I lift them
with a slotted spoon and drain them
on newspapers. Her back to me
my mother washes her hands,
letting the water run and run. The kitchen
fills with the old brown smell
of roasted cumin, crushed cilantro leaves.

Burning Bride

*for the victims
of dowry deaths
in India*

1.

In the beginning was fire,
the color of sunrise
through coconut palms,
the color of my wedding *sari*.
Festive with smell of incense,
the flames flicked playful tongues.
Stumbling to match his unfamiliar gait,
I walked with him
seven times round the fire
while wedding guests threw flowers.

The whisper of fire, secret, enigmatic,
I heard it
under the *brahmins'* rising chants,
under the *shehnai* music
flooding our bed like the molten moon.
Fire, too, his eyes, his touch.
His breath a whispered fire. And my *sari*
spilled on the floor that volcano night
redgashed, a tide of lava.

2.

The day after the wedding
they took off my jewelry, weighed it.
When it came up short
of my father's promise,
they looked at me.
Their eyes glowed pale as coals.

I wrote my father, but I knew already.
The last cow sold,
two sisters left to marry off.
There was no more for my dowry.

They got rid of the servant
who broke coals for the kitchen,
put me to work in that room, windowless,
where slabs lay piled
black on black dust.
Fire in the chest,
each indrawn breath a stabbing flame
as I strained to swing the hammer.

I wrote once more,
again knowing the reply.
If I left my husband's home
the family name would be black,
my sisters left unwed.
I did not write again.

Fire deep in the empty belly,
lying on the dark bedroom floor,
touching my wet face,
not knowing blood from tears.

Had I died,
he could have married again,
a good wife,
one with a dowry.
But though they prayed,
though we all prayed,
I did not die.

3.

I saw them bring the kerosene last night
under the thin crescent
of the failing moon.
They hid the tins
in the women's house, where we spend
the defiled days each month.
They will do it next week
when it is my time,
the dark time of my blood.

I know what happens.
Last month I saw the body
of the night-watchman's new wife.
They gave her a grand funeral,
a hundred guests.

But under the piled jasmines,
the golden sandalpaste,
was the indecent gash of pink,
the skin crisped away,
the smell of charred flesh,
unmistakable,
lodging deep in my belly.
I smell it as I wait.

Did they hold her down, struggling,
oozing the dark oily stain?
Did they silence her cries,
rough hand clamping across lips,
so the only sounds
were the sharp rasp of a match
and the quick blue hiss of fire
leaping in a night turned sudden red?

Sand blows, coarse as camel
hair against a blistered thigh.
Over the dry lake bed, heat
walls and wavers. Shrunken,
lizard-skinned, the old man
leans on his shovel. Each day
he digs in the same spot. The
hole is not deep. Each night
the *Lu* wind rolls the grains
back. His face is desert-
colored, his eyes flat as the
yellow horizon. Under the
lake bed, he says, lie the girl-
children, curled like fists.
When the water started go-
ing, they were given to the
goddess. Still the lake dried
up. The people who did not
die went to the city. The
children are not far, he as-
sures me. On windless nights
he hears their voices trickling
up, like light. Soon he will
reach them, the clean, bright
arcs of jaw bone, the amaz-
ing white hollows of the
sockets, the slivered ribs fused
into wings colored like rain.

Living Underground: Dacca 1971

The sky was a rusted lid
at the end of the tunneled night.
We learned to read
by the light of bones.
In our dreams the trees
drew in their branches,
shrank into seeds. The air
was the thin color
of smoke, frayed wings.
We pressed our ears
to the ceiling, listening
for sounds dragged off
like heavy sacks.

Each day we asked each other,
are the clouds studded
with the diamond-eyes of bats?
Are the dogs calling our names?

Family Photo in Black and White

The photographer has crowded us together
onto his one overstuffed sofa,
given us exact instructions
how to smile. You could
mistake us for a happy family,
except our spines stiffen
away from the sofa as
from a wall of ice. Mother
at one end, Father at the other,
between them, my brothers and I,
hands cupping our careful knees,
bodies gathered inward
like wounds.

The camera's flash on his glasses
obliterates his eyes. Black butterflies
are trapped in the print
of her *sari*. In two years
he will leave us, his flight
taking off for America
while she lies sedated
in a surgical ward with green walls,
the tumor inside her
like a burning seed.
Her face is as water,
still, with a dark accepting,
turned slightly, as though looking
toward the day she will wake
to a bleeding that refuses to stop,
and find him gone.

Against the backdrop,
white as a sheet of fire,
our five shadows are splayed
like fingers thrust out blackly
to ward off something:
a sudden movement seen
from an eye-corner, a splintered sound
whose meaning is not yet known.
I search that blank brilliance
for a hint, a sign which might have,
correctly divined,
made all the difference.
I look and look
till discs like blind suns
dance across my eyes,
till the children in the picture
are finally faceless.

Restroom

I push out of Customs, stumble, almost fall, legs numb from twelve hours in the plane, bladder like it's caught between the *bajra*-crushing stones they use back in the village. I hadn't known how to tell the man next to me, so large and red-faced, to move so I could go to the toilet. Even if my mouth could shape the strange guttural sounds, I couldn't have said it for the shame of it, the voices in my head, mother, grandmother, widow-aunt, telling me women did not speak of body-things.

I press my thighs together, look for him. Eight years. Will I recognize him? Will he walk briskly like the pale men streaming past me, swinging a case, a grey coat thrown over his arm? Will he know me? I shift the heavy bag from hand to hand, flex sore muscles. The thin plastic straps have cut into my fingers, a couple of nails broken from gripping the armrest, take-off time, that sharp angled rush into the sky, the houses and streets of Bombay flattened and falling away. Teeth biting down to keep in the crying, the hot bile so much worse than morning sickness. Hollow pit inside me, like after my daughter's birth. Had to leave her with my mother-in-law because he said we couldn't afford a child with us now. I'll have to work in the store all day, and who would watch her. I know how important the store is. How he saved for it, one meal a day, rice and water, washed his pants and shirt by hand each night. Now it's half his. A bad part of town, he wrote, but good money, especially in liquor. I know I'll be a good worker. I'm used to it, digging in the *bajra* fields all morning, then home to cook *chapatis* for twelve over the open wood fire, pulling water from the well through the burning afternoon. Soon we'll have enough to bring our daughter, and maybe, if God wills, we'll have another, this time a strong son to carry the family name.

But why isn't he here? And this man, so huge in his blue suit, thrusting at me a card with his picture and letters that scurry like black ants so I can't read? He's saying something. I try so hard to hear, my head hurts. I finally catch a name. His name. The word Hospital. Legs shaking so much I have to sit down on the suitcase. A gun, shiny-black, on the man's hip. He speaks slowly, very loudly, opening his mouth wide each time. Robbery. Shooting. He points to his left shoulder. Shakes his head. Not Dead. Hospital. He waits. I keep my eyes open so the redness won't cover me. Band of steel around my chest, tongue too heavy to move. He is carrying my suitcase, so I follow. Then I see the sign, WOMEN. I know what that means. Niru-ben explained it to me. I make hand-gestures to the man, pointing. He nods, OK, OK.

I've never seen anything like this before. Long lights everywhere, lines of mirrors. Taps, four, six, eight of them, faucets gleaming, the white sinks shining like in a fairytale. And the women with their bright red lips, hair short and curling around their faces in golds and browns, bare, daring honey-colored legs, their short skirts, black, maroon, the thin, thin, points of their high heels. I go into a stall, just like the others are doing. Can't figure out the lock, so I have to hold on to the door. The porcelain is cold against the backs of my thighs, but it feels so good, all that pent-up fluid leaving me in a clean rush. Soft women voices hold me, a sudden laugh, silk-rustlings. The redness is far now. The air fills with a perfume I don't know. I step out, breathe deeply, fill my lungs with it. If I can count to twenty without letting go, everything will be all right. I turn on the faucet. Water flows and flows over my hands, warm and full of light, like a blessing.

The Woman Addresses Her Sleeping Lover

*for Maya at the
Women's Shelter
in Oakland*

I lie holding you.
Under my still hand
your bones hum. I am filled
with the glistening
smell of your skin,
our mingled, melting hair.

Hard to imagine
that earlier tonight
you came at me like that,
the chair crashing to the floor,
the wine seeping its yellow way
into the rug. Your fist's arc
a blue exploding light.
Tomorrow again I will wear my scarf.
Dark glasses.

I lie holding you.
Your breath
washes the silent night like the sea,
phosphorescent,
holding back from my body the dark,
the lowering, empty sky.

I lie holding you,
loving you, wishing
you would never wake.

The Rainflies

for Champa

Always they came in the monsoon nights,
the clouds boiling angry and invisible
in the ink sky, the submerged mustard fields
sliced by lightning, its lingering
sulphur smell. Somewhere, a snapped tree
would make the power lines
go down. We huddled in the yellow quilt
with the peacock pattern
and listened to the dark,
the rushing outside
that had been the road.
The green call of frogs
rose from the swamps like vapor
and second-aunt lit a lamp,
the flame smoky, blue-yellow,
curling at the edges
like the petals
of giant winter marigolds.

And suddenly the night air
would be gauze wings, silent,
inevitable as desire.
How the light
caught the dark gleam of bodies,
pale arcs plunging to fire,
that brief gossamer blaze.

The rain would end, the huge moon
tremble in the silvered branches
of the *kadam* tree. Smell of musk
in the wet air. Far away
the night train to Pathankot
would rumble across the bridge,
its whistle spearing our child-hearts.
For a long time you kept
a bundle of clothes hidden
beneath the stairs, believing
old tales where girls
cross the seven seas on backs of elephants
to win princes. But I was the one
who left, pulled by my father's job
across the ocean. You
stayed, learned to cook
red spinach and rice, make quilts
with invisible stitches,
the tamarind-leaf design,
to bathe fully clothed
in the women's pond.

Nothing in your few letters to show
what led you one rain-swelled night
to the bridge, the tracks
gleaming fire, the whistle
slicing the night like a man's
smile. In my sleep
the vast fields fall away
from your arced body,
the gauze of your *sari*
blazes briefly white
in the train's glaring eye.
Below, water, black and endless.

The morning after the storm
the maid would sweep out
piles of pale wings, torn and shimmerless,
the blind bodies crawling
antlike in desperate circles
searching for the flame.

At Muktinath

1.

When they finally found us
aimless on the ice below the Thorong La,
stares frozen blank,
it must have been the fifth day—
or was it the sixth?
Reaching across cracks in the memory
bottomless as that crevasse, concealed, dark,
into which our young *sherpa* fell,
I connect with nothing.
One instant he was with us, laughing,
kicking up sprays of new snow
white as his teeth. Then his wail
ricocheting from rock faces.
Finally, silence.
For hours we lay with our mouths
against that black ice-mouth, breathing death.
Shone useless flashlights,
dangled rope, calling his name.
All night the mountains flung back at us
Angtarkay, Ang-tar-kay....
In the morning we had to go on.

2.

Was it the third day
we sank knee-deep in slush with every step?
Pushed ahead as in a dream, not advancing?
Surely before that was rain,
insidious fingers piercing our clothes
sharp as hypodermic needles,
bringing pain, then numb release.
Later, smoking torches, leathery *Pahari* faces,
arms around us, carrying.
Agony as they soaked our hands and feet
in steaming buckets. In between,
a woman down on snow, its blanket
waiting to enfold her in jasmine sleep.
Someone pulling at me to get up, get up.
All around, sky
spinning in blind white spheres.

They wrapped us in whatever they had—
blankets, sacks, their own yakskin coats.
In the kitchen, our backs against the stove,
they steadied our heads as we drank.
The hot tea and jaggery
flowed through me, a glowing.

3.

When I could walk again, an old woman
took me to the temple.
Together, silent, we approached the *lingam*,
inscrutable black stone
gleaming flame-ringed from the alcove.
Outside, a fountain with a cow's head.
I knelt and put my lips
against the grainy stone,
let the water fill my mouth. Its clear,
cold, mineral taste. The temple flags
fluttered like bright wings inside me.
When I opened my eyes,
beyond the calm stone profile the sky
had unfolded itself,
pulsing electric and blue,
shining as though the day would never die.

My Mother Combs My Hair

The room is full
of the scent of crushed hibiscus,
my mother's breath.
Our positions are of childhood,
I kneeling on the floor,
she crosslegged
on the chair behind.
She works the comb
through permed strands
rough as dry seaweed.
I can read regret in her fingers
untangling snarls,
rubbing red *jabakusum* oil
into brittle ends.

When she was my age,
her hair reached her knees,
fell in a thick black rush
beyond the edges
of old photographs. In one,
my father has daringly
covered her hand with his
and made her smile.
At their marriage, she told me,
because of her hair
he did not ask for a dowry.

This afternoon I wait
for the old comments,
how you've ruined your hair,
this plait's like a lizard's tail,
or, *if you don't take better care*
of it, you'll never get married.
But the braiding is done,
each strand
in its neat place, shining,
the comb put away.

I turn to her, to the grey
snaking in at the temples,
the cracks growing
at the edges of her eyes
since father left.
We hold the silence
tight between us
like a live wire,
like a strip of gold
torn from a wedding brocade.

Boychild

You lie in your grandmother's lap,
neck draped ragdoll-limp
over her wrist. Your sightless eyes
roll up at the ceiling. Drool
glistens at your ivory mouth.
Each shard of breath
pierces your clenched chest.

Your mother, my sister, will not
meet my look. The thin silk
under her eyes is bruised with waking.
On her forehead, vermillion powder
to bring you luck, around her upper arm
a large bronze amulet, mate
to the one that pulls at your neck.

They made her wear it
on her twenty-first birthday,
two months after the tests revealed
you curled inside her, motionless,
your brain drowning in milky fluid.
Abort, the doctor told her.
But your father
refused. First boychild,
bearer of the family name,
you could not be so easily released.

Your father's parents spoke
of miracle shrines
in their Gujarat village,

magic childbirth-stones. Wires were sent,
horoscopes shouted
over long-distance phones.
The astrologers found your mother's planets
bad, Saturn rising
in the sixth house. They mailed her
holy ashes, vials of temple-water,
the amulets for your cure.
Still you came cryless,
blind albino fish into lung-scalding light.

Eighteen times in your eight-month life
the ambulance shrieked the night-road,
rushed you crumpled and blue
and burning as a star
where oxygen-tents cobwebbed you,
the thick tubes bled your mouth,
needles glittered in translucent flesh.

Now you are briefly home.
Around you the women listen
to your lungs' desperate, gurgling suck.
Your airless world
unwings the bright words I brought. They drop
like crippled birds into my lap.
I crush them in my fists and wish you death.

My Mother at Maui

The plumeria's narcotic perfume
dizzied you, its indecent
lushness. You shunned the rows
of gleaming flesh at the beach.
No extra rooms available, you dragged
your mattress to the balcony
each night, even when the weather turned,
appearing in the morning with
an accusing cough.

One evening, dinner hour,
I persuaded you to the deserted
ocean. Fully clothed,
even your glasses, you hesitated
at the water's edge, then plunged in
with a kind of desperation. The sun's long
red finger trembled to touch you.
When the wave rushed up and threw itself
on you, you reared back, then dived in
to chase the foam.
Your *sari* billowed around you,
a white petalling. Mother,
on your face a look I had not seen
even before father left,
as though a child, long-drowned,
had struggled up through years of oozy dark
and breathed the opal light.

After a while, you remembered me,
returned to shore,
shivering a little. I wrapped
the towel around your shoulders.
We walked back, silent, your hand
light as a nesting bird
in the oval of my arm.

The Garland

They had been married almost ten years when he said, *you are a good woman so I'd rather you heard this from me than through servant-gossip. I'm bringing home the daughter of Jalal Mohammed as my new wife.*

She kept her eyes on the square mosaic pattern of the floor till he left. The law allowed him four wives. Two pregnancies and two miscarriages, her body with its scarred, stretched skin no longer excited him. She had given him no male heir. If he said the word divorce three times, *talaq, talaq, talaq,* she would be out on the street with her daughters. She knew all this.

She went about her daily business calmly. Not a tremor crossed her face when she heard people say, *Jalal Mohammed's daughter had skin like honey, eyes like black sapphires.* If in her room she screamed, pounded the floor with her fists, banged her forehead against its coldness till the blood came, if one afternoon she twisted her *sari* tight into a rope and tied it to the ceiling hook and watched its swaying for a long time before she untied it, no one knew.

Everyone said, *by all the angels of Allah, a woman should be like this.* Her husband was relieved. A hysterical woman in the house was such an inconvenience, especially when one was preparing for a wedding. He gave her a gold chain as gift, and when she asked if she could decorate the marriage-bed, he was happy to allow her, for she was known for her skill with flowers.

The new bride walked into a forest of blossoms—brass jars full of marigolds and crimson roses, branches of oleanders hanging from the ceiling, thick ropes of jasmine snaking around bedposts. On the white satin pillow was a garland just large enough to fit around a woman's throat. Not recognizing the iridescent petals, the bride picked it up. It was light as a breath in her hand, and some of the satin dust rubbed off on her fingertips. She saw—the woman must have been collecting them for weeks—it was made of torn butterfly wings.

The House

Wrinkled and shrunk, like father
before his death, it leans
rusty windowbars into the thick
honeysuckle. Thorny bougainvillaea,
heaped over balconies, glows
blood in the sunset. I wade
through bleached dry grass that crackles
around my thighs, shatter the old padlock

with a rock. Inside, dark sounds
scuttle and flap.
No one knows I'm here.
My uncles and aunts, my fiancé,
are busy back in town
fixing the wedding date.
They would never have let me come.

I slide through the crack.
Cobwebs cling to my face,
mildewed silk. In the grey light,
as if underwater, I search for hours.
My shoes crunch through bat skeletons,
their paper wings. Sharp-toothed rodents
guide me with skittering claws
to chests filled with bedtime tales
and old shoes. Cupboards, opened,
spill tears like diamonds.
At last I see it in the corner,
tiny, glowing firefly-bright:

my childhood, just as I left it.
I reach out but there's a sharp
hiss. Between us, an enormous cobra,
hood upraised, black
as my father's eyes.
I lunge. Fall. The cobra strikes.
Poison burns blue
up my veins. The shell of the house
cracks open around me. I feel my body
begin to float up into night air.
In my cupped palm my childhood
pulses light. The cobra coils
like a ribbon of silk in my hair.

The Gift

They are singing the wedding song
of the good woman. Firecrackers
explode like hearts across a blind
and wheeling sky. In this bedroom
already emptied of my girlhood, I stand
in front of the mirror. The heavy red
of bride-silks weighs me down, gold
pulls at my wrists, my ears. I open
the box. Against worn black velvet
the pearls are globes of fire,
my mother's gift.

> *A good woman is a lamp*
> *brightening her mother's name*

Light from the candle shudders on the pearls,
each strand a rope of shining. Outside,
a *shehnai* wails as the groom
steps over our threshold. I picture
his *kurta*, the starched silk
color of bone, the face I have seen
only in pictures.

> *A good woman is known*
> *by her silent, serving hands.*

Hard, white, the pearls press
into my face, chill
as her wet cheekbone night
after splintered night. Mornings,
she hid in the folds of her *sari*
the blotches, yellow, purple,
erupting under the eye.

*A good woman regards
her husband as her god.*

Incense from the wedding fire
is thick, eye-watering. It is time
for me to walk behind him
around the sacred flames. Time
to speak my wedding vows, to put
my hand into his.

*A good woman leaves her husband's home
only for the cremation grounds.*

They are knocking on the door. The air
is full of drums, crushed jasmine,
cries like birds. Someone
calls my name. Mother, I clasp your gift
around my throat. See how well it fits,
each beautiful, burning strand.

Villagers Visiting Jodhpur Enjoy Iced Sweets

after a photograph by Raghubir Singh

In their own village they would never dare it,
these five men, sitting on the grainy grey sand
by the roadside tea stall, licking at ices.
Against their brown mouths the ices are
an impossible orange, like childhood fires.
They do not look at each other, do not speak.
One man has loosened his headgear
and lets it hang around his neck.
Another, crosslegged,
grasps his ice with earnest hands.
A third takes a tiny bite from the side,
willing it not to melt. The *Lu* wind
wrenches at the fronds of date-palms,
rasps the men's faces. But inside, the ices
are cool and heavy on the tongue,
on throats raw from cursing
the moneylender for unpayable debts,
the gods for the rainless, burning fields.

Soon, dust-choked, the village bus will come.
The men will board, wiping their tinted mouths
secretly on *dhoti*-edges. Back home,
heads of households, they will beat
wives and children as necessary, get drunk
at the toddy-feasts. Their fields

seized, they will hold their heads high
and visit the local whorehouse. But for now,
held within these frozen orange crystals,
silent, sucking,
they have forgotten to be men.

Visit

I peel off your plastic underwear,
wipe the damp crud crusting folds of skin.
My fingers probe where a daughter
should never go. I try
to gentle them but you flinch away
and will not look at me. Your shame
fills the room, rusty odor
of urine, the stains
down the front of your robe.

The bathing takes so long, wrinkle
by wrinkle, hair by matted hair.
Your breasts sagging into tepid water.
The large circles of washcloth
on armpit and thigh. You close
your eyes and mouth, pale
tight slits, against me. When
I lift you out, porous, weightless,
and wrap you in towels,
you cannot stop the shaking.

Through the meal I talk and talk
to fill the hollows of your bones
with my futile voice. You part
your lips, obedient to my spoon:
mashed potatoes, strained carrot soup,
soaked bread. Perhaps a boiled egg
tonight, I ask, apples chopped fine,
cooked soft. I show you pictures

of my daughters—birthdays, visits
to the zoo. You smile
at the bright shapes, then look
through me. The skin around your eyes
creases in concentration
at something I cannot see.

If I told you that tonight
I must pack your things, that tomorrow
they will take you to Sunnyside Manor,
would you know to weep?
To remember how at Gorakhpur
when your father broke his hip,
you kept him with you? Year after year
cleaned the bedsores opening their mouths
like red flowers?
To ask why I cannot?

There is so much I have no answers for:
why the cloudless afternoon
outside your window is jagged
by lightning and a sound so fierce
you hold your head and moan.
Why I bend into the floor's grime
and scrub, teeth clamped, until I ache,
jaw and nail and knee. Why
seeing again the forgotten blue tiles

of your kitchen, your eyes fill
in this phenol air, raw stinging whiff
of cadaver labs. Why as the dark
seeps around your bed you at last
grip my hand hard, not letting go,
as though forever were a possible truth.

Journey

On the third day the land begins to turn,
rocks and leaves the jaundiced yellow
of an animal eye. The train jolts us
toward your village across brown rivers
banked with frayed *kash* grasses. You
tell the children stories
out of your boyhood, how your father
the *zamindar* kept by his pillow
a whip made of a stingray's tail,
how he used it on the woman
the villagers found in the fields
with a man not her husband,
and sometimes on you.
The weals on your back still rise
in ridges, reddish, puckered.
Sometimes when you are slumped
against me in sleep, I touch them.

The great hall with the chandeliers
was filled with stuffed heads
from your father's hunts:
tiger, buffalo, antelope,
the huge glaring rhino, horn still stained,
that split his leg open.
At night when you slept they slid
silent, legless, down the walls
to prowl the corridor's dark.
The night your father heard you say this
he thrust you into that room
and locked the door. You were seven.

Outside a sunset like blood
or burning grass. Shadows stamped
on the ridges of your cheekbones
stark as these broken passing hills.
The dark o's of the children's mouths.
You have no stories of your mother.
What did she do that night,
your fist thudding the black
mahogany, your torn, bleeding nails,
your sobs dying at last
into the musty odor of fur and vomit?

Night of no stars. Rushing wings outside
the blurry window. I think we are
the only people on this train,
in this world, plunging backward
into nightmare. The boy flinches
as a moth flies at his face.
You speak sharp, too loud, and
he flinches again. Your accent
is thicker, different, words
I never heard you use before.
When you go to the toilet
I want to pull the emergency chain,
run with the children to the sane
walled light of my home. Too late.
You are back, your left leg
dragging a little, like your father's,
or is it the train's lurching?

He died hunting, you and he alone
in the tall buffalo grass,
a sudden movement, a shot.
A sad accident, everyone said.

You swing the children into the upper bunks
though they are white-faced
it is so high and the train
tunnels so fast through the shapeless dark.
Switch off the dim bulb.
Now night takes us, the train's
iron noises. Tomorrow we will enter
the places of your childhood.
You will stride ahead with your son,
I, veiled and wifely, with your daughter
behind. Journey's end. And when the boy
cries out from nausea or a dream, you stop me
from going to him, your grasp hard
above my elbow, your fingers
gnarled and biting down
like the roots of the giant banyan
outside your father's house.

The Durga Batik

It is fitting
that the ten-armed goddess
should be redandblack,
color of the birth canal, color also
of your dying. Red
cascades down her back, meteor hair
boiling as the wax
that etched each tendril.
Her black breast
is shaped like night
in the Bengal hills
where a batik must be dipped
at the exact hour
when mosquitoes sing like stars.
A lion crouches
at her right foot. You see
in its ruby stare
that she can fly
wingless, can all at once
hang here redandblack
as a monsoon cloud,
and glide, dark moon,
on phosphorus swamps in Sundarban
where the clay glows flamewhite
as the serrated edge of her spear,
white as her eyes,
the far gaze you plunge into,
color of your first memory, color also
of what over and over
you have forgotten.

Glossary

Alarippu Classical Indian dance, usually occurs at the beginning of a performance.

amma Mother.

Angrezi English, Western.

ayah Maidservant, midwife, nanny.

Baisakh Month corresponding to April.

bajra Coarse wheat-like grain (sorghum).

barfi Milk-based solid dessert, often rectangular.

brahmin A member of the priest caste.

bulbul Red-crested songbird, nightingale.

burkha Robe and veil, usually black, worn by Muslim women over regular clothing.

chai Tea.

chamar Man belonging to the untouchable caste.

chapati Rolled-out bread, similar to tortillas.

chappal Footwear, sandal.

choli Woman's upper garment, similar to a blouse.

dhoti Man's lower garment, a single piece of cloth tied around the waist.

Dandia Indian folk dance.

Diwali Festival of Lights.

dupatta Woman's scarf.

Garba Indian folk dance.

ghat Bathing area on the bank of a river or pond, usually segregated by sex.

godhuli Evening hour considered auspicious for weddings (literally, cow-dust; twilight, or the time the cows are driven home).

gul-mohur Tree with orange and yellow blossoms.

jabakusum Hair-oil made from hibiscus flowers.

kadam   Tree with large ball-like fragrant flowers that blossom during the monsoon season.

kaju   Cashew.

kameez   Woman's tunic.

karela   Bitter melon.

kash   Long wild grass with white flowers.

Kumari   Virgin Goddess.

kumkum   Red paste or powder used for weddings or prayer rituals.

kurta   Man's loose tunic.

laddu   Ball-shaped dessert.

lingam   Stone idol representing Shiva (phallic).

Lu   Hot desert wind.

matar-panir   Curry made with hard cheese (ricotta, pressed) and peas.

methi   Fenugreek.

Nataraja   Classical Indian dance, usually occurs at the end of a performance.

Navaratri   Nine-day festival of the Goddess, held in October.

paan   Betel leaf.

Pahari   Having physical characteristics of that hill tribe.

puja   Prayer ceremony.

roti   Like *chapati*, a rolled-out bread.

saag   Spinach.

salwar   Loose pants for women.

sari   Long piece of cloth wrapped around the body, worn by women all over India.

sati   A woman who immolates herself on her husband's funeral pyre. The word literally means "good woman."

shal Tree with large, sturdy leaves (kind of teak).
shehnai Oboe-like instrument played at weddings.
Sheora Tree associated with evil spirits.
sherpa Mountain-guide belonging to a hill tribe.
tabla Indian drums.
talaq Urdu word meaning "I divorce you."
Tillana Classical Indian dance.
zamindar Landowner.

About the Author

Originally from India, **Chitra Banerjee Divakaruni** lives in the San Francisco Bay Area, where she teaches Creative Writing at Foothill College. She has a Ph.D. in English from the University of California at Berkeley (1984) and an M.A. from Wright State University, Dayton, Ohio (1978).

Her work has appeared in *CALYX, A Journal of Art and Literature by Women; Woman of Power; Z Miscellaneous; Amelia; Berkeley Poets Co-op Magazine; Beloit Poetry Journal; Colorado Review; Folio; Occident; Nexus; Primavera; thirteen; Threepenny Review; Kingfisher; Snowy Egret; Miscellany* (India); and various anthologies. She has published two other books of poetry: *Dark Like the River* (Writers' Workshop, Calcutta, India, 1987) and *The Reason for Nasturtiums* (Berkeley Poets Press, 1990).

Divakaruni has received various poetry awards, including the Editor's Choice Award from *Cream City Review* (1991), the Santa Clara Arts Council Poetry Award (1990), nomination for the Pushcart Prize (1989-90), the Barbara Deming Memorial Award (1989), the Cecil Hackney Poetry Prize (1988), and the Nexus Award (1978).

Selected Titles from Award-Winning CALYX Books

Ginseng and Other Tales from Manila, by Marianne Villanueva. Poignant short stories set in the Philippines.
ISBN 0-934971-19-6, $8.95, paper; ISBN 0-934971-20-X, $16.95, cloth.

Idleness Is the Root of All Love, by Christa Reinig, translated by Ilze Mueller. These poems by the prize-winning German poet accompany two older lesbians through a year together in love and struggle.
ISBN 0-934971-21-8, $10, paper; ISBN 0-934971-22-6, $18.95, cloth.

The Forbidden Stitch: An Asian American Women's Anthology, edited by Shirley Geok-lin Lim, et. al. The first Asian American women's anthology. **Winner of the American Book Award.**
ISBN 0-934971-04-8, $16.95, paper; ISBN 0-934971-10-2, $29.95, cloth.

Women and Aging, An Anthology by Women, edited by Jo Alexander, et. al. The only anthology that addresses ageism from a feminist perspective. A rich collection of older women's voices.
ISBN 0-934971-00-5, $15.95, paper; ISBN 0-934971-07-2, $28.95, cloth.

In China with Harpo and Karl, by Sibyl James. Essays revealing a feminist poet's experiences while teaching in Shanghai, People's Republic of China.
ISBN 0-934971-15-3, $9.95, paper; ISBN 0-934971-16-1, $17.95, cloth.

Indian Singing in 20th Century America, by Gail Tremblay. A work of hope by a Native American poet.
ISBN 0-934971-13-7, $8.95, paper; ISBN 0-934971-14-5, $16.95, cloth.

The Riverhouse Stories, by Andrea Carlisle. A classic! Unlike any other lesbian novel published. A delight!
ISBN 0-934971-01-3, $8.95, paper; ISBN 0-934971-08-0, $16.95, cloth.

Forthcoming Titles – 1992

Killing Color, by Charlotte Watson Sherman. These compelling, mythical short stories by a gifted storyteller delicately explore the African-American experience.
ISBN 0-934971-17-X, $8.95, paper; ISBN 0-934971-18-8, $16.95, cloth.

Mrs. Vargas and the Dead Naturalist, by Kathleen Alcalá. Fourteen stories set in Mexico and the Southwestern US, written in the tradition of magical realism.
ISBN 0-934971-25-0, $9.95, paper; ISBN 0-934971-26-9, $18.95, cloth.

The Nicaraguan Women Poets Anthology, edited by Daisy Zamora. A collection of poetry by Nicaraguan women—Miskito Indian women, early 20th century poets, and better-known poets writing since the 1960s.
ISBN 0-934971-27-7, paper; ISBN 0-934971-28-5, cloth. Prices pending.

CALYX Books is committed to producing books of literary, social, and feminist integrity.

These books are available at your local bookstore or direct from:

CALYX Books, PO Box B, Corvallis, OR 97339

(Please include payment with your order. Add $1.50 postage for first book and $.75 for each additional book.)

CALYX, Inc., is a nonprofit organization
with a 501(C)(3) status.
All donations are tax deductible.

The text of this book is composed in Janson Text.
Titles are in Present.
Composition by ImPrint Services, Corvallis, Oregon.